THE REAL STORY
OF THE 1914
CHRISTMAS TRUCE

by David James Ault
and Dr. Tara Tempus

A Time Immemorial History Book

Time School
History just got interesting

FOREWORD

Dear reader,

Although I had studied World War I in quite some detail during my 5th Year at Time Immemorial High, I was not aware of any Christmas Truce until I actually saw it happen with my own eyes.

Those of you who have followed my travels through time will of course know that it was actually my first trip using a time band, and it is certainly an event in history that has fascinated me ever since.

Those of you who are less familiar with my early days as a time traveller are able to read about my exploits in 1914 through a fictionalised account by David James Ault, in his book, *Time School*, which on the whole is a faithful interpretation of what took place.

The book that you are about to read, however, is in no way a work of fiction. I have painstakingly researched the events leading up to and following the Christmas Truce, as well as commentaries and reports in the media up to and including the centenary, in 2014.

* * *

David then used this same research to write this book and also to create an online history course, entitled "World War I: The Christmas Truce of 1914", which is definitely worth checking out, especially as readers of this book are entitled to a substantial discount on the regular price.

While it is of paramount importance that we never forget the horrors of World War One, I believe it is just as important to remember those wonderful moments in history where, despite overwhelming odds, man's humanity is able to shine, even if it is only for a fleeting moment. And in particular, as Sir Arthur Conan Doyle sensibly noted, we should marvel at this *'one human episode amid all the atrocities, which have stained the memory of the war'*.

Yours throughout time,

Tempus

Dr. Tara Tempus

London, Europe, 2264.

PREFACE

The horrors of World War I were such that following the conflict President Woodrow Wilson was moved enough to boldly promise that it would be the war to end all wars. Although that particular prophecy was short-lived, the Great War is still seen today as one of mankind's darkest hours and the most recognisable symbol for the futility of war.

Nonetheless, during that period of hell on earth, there was one brief moment when man's humanity and desire for peace shone through. And even though the Christmas Truce was only to last a few days, never to be repeated, it remains a beacon of hope, amongst all the hopelessness that is war.

This account of the Christmas Truce actually begins with the road to war, covering a number of the factors that ultimately led to World War I. This is followed by a look at the early months of the war, trench warfare, other unofficial armistices throughout history and also early attempts at a truce in the December of 1914.

The Christmas Truce itself is then discussed, looking in turn at the events that took place on Christmas Eve, Christmas Day and Boxing Day, in 1914, before examining the part that football may have played within the truce.

Finally, the legacy of the Christmas Truce is considered,

especially in the context of the centenary celebrations of 2014, and why football has become the overriding symbol for the truce in modern times.

Throughout the book, I have tried to include some interesting "Did You Know?" snippets of information, and there is actually a quiz at the end of each chapter, so that you, the reader, are able to test your knowledge as you go along.

I would like to take this opportunity to thank you for purchasing "The Real Story of the 1914 Christmas Truce" and I hope that you find the book both enjoyable and educational.

You might also be interested in checking out "World War I: The Christmas Truce of 1914", which is a brand new online course that I recently put together. Please note that the readers of this book are entitled to a substantial discount on the price of the course.

CHAPTER ONE

The Road to War

A POWDER KEG WAITING TO EXPLODE

By 1914, Europe had become a hotbed of alliances and political intrigue. Two nations in particular stood out: Germany, an economic Goliath, with the largest army in the world, and Great Britain, who still very much ruled the waves and had built an empire that even Germany was envious of.

Royal family ties did not seem to make the uneasiness in Europe any better; if anything they probably made the situation worse. Three cousins now held the power in Europe: King George V, Kaiser Wilhelm II and Tsar Nicholas II, and although the British King and Russian Tsar had quite a warm relationship, the same could not be said of their German cousin, Wilhelm.

* * *

2

The Christmas Truce of 1914

Queen Victoria's attempt to ensure peace through family matchmaking in the 19th Century seemed to have badly backfired. Her eldest grandson, Wilhelm had grown up resenting all things British, in particular George's father, King Edward VII. The Kaiser's jealousy towards his uncle Edward had certainly helped spur him on to build such a great army, as well as the building of a navy, which he hoped would one day rival the Royal Navy.

Wilhelm had also been furious with his uncle for seemingly encircling Germany within a web of alliances, the most noticeable of which was the entente cordiale, a series of agreements signed on the 8th April 1904, between Britain and France. When added to the Franco-Russian Alliance of 1892, it is understandable to see Wilhelm's concerns of being boxed in.

Meanwhile, Germany's strongest ally was fast becoming her greatest liability. The once mighty Austro-Hungarian Empire was beginning to weaken, both militarily and economically. Furthermore, it was involved in a number of border disputes with the Balkan countries, which were becoming embarrassing to Austria-Hungary, and in turn to Germany itself.

In particular, Serbia was becoming a thorn in the Austrian emperor's side, with terrorist groups causing trouble at every turn. This was now coming to a head, with Germany strongly advising Austria-Hungary to keep their house in order and solve the Serbian problem.

* * *

It was perhaps surprising then that it was not in Serbia, but in neighbouring Bosnia, that an incident took place, which was to ignite the powder keg that Europe had become and trigger a series of seemingly unstoppable events, which would lead not only to a war in Europe, but eventually to the first ever world war.

Did you know?

In 1914, Austria-Hungary was made up from the following ethnic groups:

Germans, Hungarians, Czechs, Slovaks, Poles, Ukrainians, Slovenes, Croats, Serbs, Romanians and Italians.

THE ARCHDUKE FRANZ FERDINAND

The Archduke Franz Ferdinand had always been somewhat of an embarrassment to his uncle, Franz Joseph, the Emperor of Austria-Hungary. His playboy lifestyle did not go down at all well with the Emperor, especially when Franz Ferdinand became heir to his throne, in 1896. However, it was Franz Ferdinand's marriage to Sophie Chotek, which particularly infuriated his uncle.

The Emperor had made it quite clear that his nephew was not to marry Sophie, a mere countess, as it was contrary to the rules of the Habsburg family, who were only permitted to marry a member of one of the European royal dynasties. Franz Ferdinand, who was totally besotted with Sophie, ignored his uncle's wishes.

* * *

Emperor Franz Joseph did finally allow the marriage to go ahead, in 1901, thanks in part to a request from Kaiser Wilhelm, who was a close friend of Franz Ferdinand, but only on the proviso that the marriage would be morganatic, which meant that their descendants would not have any succession rights to the throne.

As it turned out, Sophie would be a good influence over Franz Ferdinand's life and over time even the rift with his uncle had healed enough that he began to take an active role in the government and carry out official engagements. It was on one such engagement in the summer of 1914 that he found himself in Sarajevo, the capital of Bosnia.

The Archduke must have been aware of how dangerous such

a trip was. His uncle had been the subject of a failed assassination attempt by the Serbian secret military society, Unification or Death, also known as the 'Black Hand', a few years earlier, in 1911. However, despite the known risks, Franz Ferdinand and his wife, Sophie, drove through the streets of Sarajevo on the 28th June 1914, in an open sports motorcar with its top folded down.

The security provided for the Archduke while he was in Sarajevo was altogether quite lax. A proposal that troops line the route was dismissed out of hand, as it was believed that this would offend the loyal citizens of Bosnia. With hindsight, this lack of security was extremely foolhardy, as the assassination of the Archduke had actually been in the planning since March of that year.

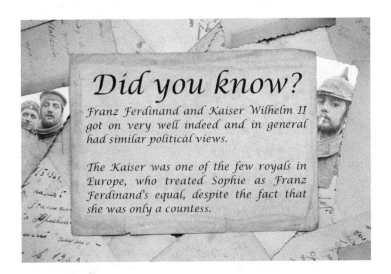

Did you know?

Franz Ferdinand and Kaiser Wilhelm II got on very well indeed and in general had similar political views.

The Kaiser was one of the few royals in Europe, who treated Sophie as Franz Ferdinand's equal, despite the fact that she was only a countess.

AN UNLIKELY ASSASSINATION

On the morning of the 28th June 1914, a team of six assassins had been assembled in Sarajevo by Danilo Ilić, a Bosnian Orthodox Serb, who was a member of the Black Hand secret society. The assassins, who had been trained in Serbia, were armed with bombs and pistols and had been posted along the motorcade route of the Archduke. The team consisted of five Serbs and a Bosniak by the name of Gavrilo Princip.

The series of events leading up to the assassination really were quite remarkable and from the outset it appeared that the dastardly act was all set to fail. The motorcade passed the first two assassins without either of them acting, but the third would-be assassin, a Serb called Nedeljko Čabrinović, threw his bomb at the motorcar that Franz Ferdinand and Sophie were driving in. However, the bomb actually bounced off the folded back cover of the convertible sports car and exploded under the next car in the motorcade, injuring about 20 people in the process.

The rest of the cars then sped up, which meant that the three remaining assassins, including the sole Bosniak, Gavrilo Princip, each failed to act as the Archduke's car passed them by. Meanwhile, Čabrinović had swallowed a cyanide tablet and then jumped into the Miljacka river, in order to avoid being captured. Incredibly, he did not die, as the cyanide tablet was past its sell-by date, only making him sick, and the river was not very deep during the summer months. Instead, he was arrested by the police, but not before being badly beaten by an angry crowd.

Having escaped the assassination attempt unscathed, Franz Ferdinand and Sophie continued on with their visit to the Town Hall, where the Archduke was scheduled to give a speech. Clearly shaken by the events, he began his speech by saying, *"Mr. Mayor, I came here on a visit and I am greeted with bombs. It is outrageous"*.

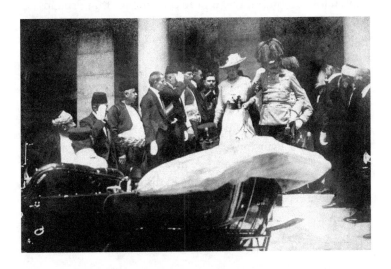

Archduke Franz Ferdinand and Sophie in Sarajevo 5 minutes before the assassination

(Creative Commons 3.0: attribution Karl Tröstl, via www.Europeana1914-1918.eu)

After the reception, the Archduke decided that rather than

continuing with the planned itinerary, he and Sophie would instead go and visit the victims injured in the attack. For security reasons, a change in the route was decided upon in order to avoid the city centre. Unfortunately, the chauffeur driving Franz Ferdinand's car did not know the new route and made a wrong turn down a side street.

As fate would have it, they had driven down the very same street that Gavrilo Princip happened to be waiting on. It is not known for certain if it was a pure coincidence that Princip was stood outside of Moritz Schiller's Delicatessen, or if he believed the street to be part of the Archduke's return route from the Town Hall.

Whatever the reason, Gavrilo Princip had found himself in the right place at the right time. As the chauffeur fumbled with the gears, Princip was able to walk up to the car and fire two shots from less than six feet away; hitting Franz Ferdinand in the neck and Sophie in the stomach. They both died before receiving any medical assistance.

* * *

At his trial, Princip later confessed that he had only meant to shoot the Archduke and was truly sorry that Sophie had also been murdered. Aged nineteen, Princip was too young to receive the death penalty for his crime and so was given the maximum sentence of 20 years in prison, where he died of tuberculosis, almost four years later.

* * *

As horrible as this deed in Sarajevo had been, no-one could possibly have envisaged the series of events that followed. Whether or not the assassination was just used as an excuse for war, which Germany in particular pounced upon, there is no doubting the fact that the assassination in Sarajevo was the straw that broke the camel's back.

POLITICS AND INTRIGUE

Following the assassination of the Archduke, events took place at a frightening rate. Emperor Franz Joseph was outraged that his nephew had been killed and demanded quick retribution, but the once mighty Austria-Hungary declaring war on lowly Serbia was not as easy as it may have appeared and Emperor Franz Joseph knew fine well he would need Kaiser Wilhelm's permission.

Kaiser Wilhelm himself was deeply saddened at his friend's

murder, but he was warned by his ministers that Serbia had a powerful ally of it's own in Russia. They knew that if Austria-Hungary went to war with Serbia, there was a very strong chance that Russia would declare war on Austria-Hungary. Then Emperor Franz Joseph would no doubt come to Germany and ask the Kaiser for help against Russia. And a war with Russia was also not without its complications.

Russia had a longstanding alliance with France, which had been established for the very purpose of ensuring that the German powerhouse would not go to war with either country. Although Germany had by far the strongest army and stockpile of weapons, it would mean the possibility of a war on two fronts. A situation that the German ministers were strongly advising the Kaiser not to even contemplate.

And there were further complications, which the German government were all too ready to point out to their Kaiser. According to the Schlieffen Plan, the only successful way of defeating France was to invade them via Belgium. And the German ministers strongly advised the Kaiser against doing that, as Belgium just so happened to have an alliance with Great Britain.

Incredibly, the Kaiser refused to take the advice of his own government and actively encouraged his cousin Franz Joseph to declare war on Serbia. It is not known exactly whether Kaiser Wilhelm hoped that the alliances would not hold up, or whether he actually felt that Germany was strong enough to take on the whole of Europe on two fronts.

The Christmas Truce of 1914

* * *

Whatever his reasoning, Austria-Hungary's declaration of war against Serbia on the 28th July 1914 led to a series of unstoppable events, and on the 4th August 1914, only 37 days after the assassination of Archduke Franz Ferdinand, Great Britain declared war on Germany citing as the reason the violation of the The Treaty of London, in which Belgium's neutrality was to be respected by all nations.

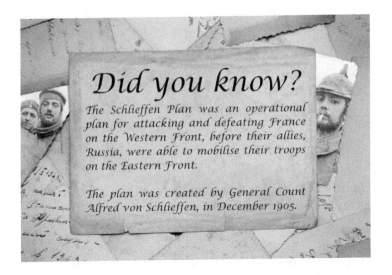

Did you know?

The Schlieffen Plan was an operational plan for attacking and defeating France on the Western Front, before their allies, Russia, were able to mobilise their troops on the Eastern Front.

The plan was created by General Count Alfred von Schlieffen, in December 1905.

TEST YOUR KNOWLEDGE IN THE

What have you learnt about the road to war?

(N.B. The answers are shown on the following page)

Question One: Name Kaiser Wilhelm II's two cousins, who were also kings of their countries?

Question Two: What were the series of agreements signed between Britain and France commonly called?

Question Three: In what year did the Archduke Franz Ferdinand finally marry Sophie?

* * *

Question Four: What is the capital of Bosnia?

Question Five: What is the Serbian secret military society, Unification or Death, more commonly known as?

Question Six: Who was the sole Bosniak on the team of assassins?

Question Seven: Near to which delicatessen was the Archduke assassinated?

Question Eight: How old was Gavrilo Princip when he assassinated the Archduke?

Question Nine: Strategically, what country did Germany need to invade to defeat France?

Question Ten: On what date did Great Britain declare war on Germany?

HERE ARE THE CORRECT

Q1) King George V and Tsar Nicholas II

Q2) The entente cordiale

Q3) 1901

Q4) Sarajevo

Q5) Black Hand

Q6) Gavrilo Princip

Q7) Moritz Schiller's Delicatessen

Q8) 19

Q9) Belgium

Q10) 4th August 1914

CHAPTER TWO

The First Few Months of the War

THE WESTERN FRONT

Having declared war on Germany, Britain quickly made a formal alliance with France, a country with whom she long had an understanding through the entente cordiale, and in doing so The Triple Entente of Britain, France and Russia was born.

Meanwhile, the Ottoman Empire became part of the Triple Alliance of Central Powers, along with Germany and Austria-Hungary, after signing the Turco-German Alliance, in August 1914. The Triple Entente did not officially declare war on the Ottoman Empire until the 4th November, following the bombing of the Russian Black Sea ports.

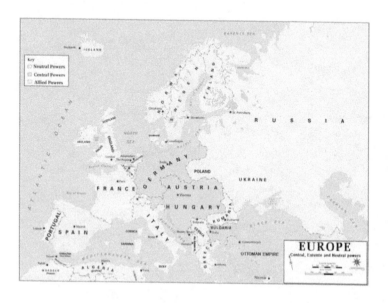

The Christmas Truce of 1914

* * *

The war on the Eastern front saw the central powers of Germany, Austria-Hungary, Bulgaria and the Ottoman Empire, fight against Russia and Romania. However, this book is specifically concerned with events that took place on the Western Front, where Germany fought against Great Britain and France, as well as Belgium, Portugal, the Dominion Forces of the British Empire (Australia, Canada, India, New Zealand, Newfoundland and South Africa) and, from April 1918, the United States of America.

The war on the Western Front began with an advance by Germany, using a modified version of the Schlieffen Plan to invade France via Luxembourg and Belgium. Although Germany was able to occupy Luxembourg without opposition on the 2nd August 1914, Belgium proved to be far more resilient than the German army had expected. Nonetheless, by the end of August, the Germans had swept through Belgium and had begun their march into Northern France, where they met with both the French army and an initial six divisions of the British Expeditionary Force.

Initially, the German army won a number of key battles, which allowed them to advance into France, gaining control of important industrial regions as they went and coming within 70 km of Paris. However, an Allied victory at the Battle of the Marne dramatically turned the tide, forcing the Germans back and setting the stage for four years of trench warfare along the Western Front.

* * *

Did you know?

The first battle of World War I was the Battle of Liège. It was also the opening engagement of the invasion of Belgium.

Germany expected to take Liège in only two days, but in fact the brave Belgian soldiers managed to withhold the German army for as long as eleven days.

A NEW TYPE OF WAR

Following the Battle of the Marne, in September 1914, both sides desperately attempted to outflank the enemy to the north in a series of manoeuvres, which became known as the "Race to the Sea". This eventually resulted in a meandering line of fortified trenches, which stretched from the Swiss border with France in the south, all the way up to the North Sea in the north. This line of trenches would pretty much remain unchanged for the rest of the war.

Trench warfare had been born, a new type of war which was totally different to any before or since. The reason that both sides dug in along these defensive lines was mainly to do with the technology at that time. It just so happens that when the war broke out, the technological advances in firepower far outweighed the advances made in mobility. This meant that the defender now held a huge advantage over the attacker and so it made sense for an army to fortify their current position and defend it.

* * *

The trenches were dug by one of three common methods, known as entrenching, sapping, and tunnelling: Entrenching was when the men would dig downwards from the surface and although it was the most efficient way of digging, it was also the most dangerous as the men were exposed above ground to sniper fire.

Sapping was where one or two diggers extended the trench by digging away at the end of it. This was a safer way of digging than entrenching, but also a much slower process. Finally, tunnelling was similar to sapping, but was even safer, due to the fact that a "roof" of soil was left in place until the trench had been dug out.

The early trenches were simple and were packed with men

fighting shoulder to shoulder. In addition to the trenches themselves, barbed wire was placed in front, in order to improve the defences. After a few months, these small, improvised trenches began to grow deeper and more complex, eventually becoming vast areas of interlocking defensive works. These trenches were now usually about 12 ft in depth and were able to resist artillery bombardments, as well as infantry assaults.

The area between the two sets of trenches was known as no man's land and was typically between 100 and 300 yards wide. However, there were certain places on the Western Front, such as on Vimy Ridge, where the opposing troops only had as little as 30 yards of no man's land separating them.

Although conditions in the trenches were dreadful, morale was actually still quite high at this stage in the war. Supplies at the front were still in abundance and many of the lower ranked soldiers found that they ate better than they would have done back home. That said, the number of deaths among the soldiers was certainly taking its toll.

* * *

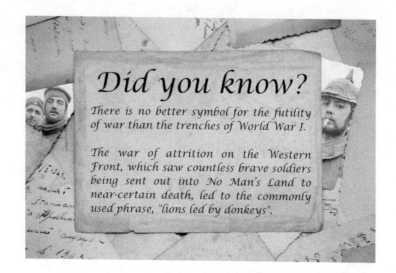

Did you know?

There is no better symbol for the futility of war than the trenches of World War I.

The war of attrition on the Western Front, which saw countless brave soldiers being sent out into No Man's Land to near-certain death, led to the commonly used phrase, "lions led by donkeys".

TEST YOUR KNOWLEDGE IN THE

What have you learnt about the First Few Months of the War?

(N.B. The answers are shown on the following page)

Question One: Which three countries made up the The Triple Entente?

Question Two: Which three countries made up the Triple Alliance of Central Powers?

Question Three: Germany used a modified version of what plan to invade France?

* * *

Question Four: The German army got within how many kilometres of Paris?

Question Five: An allied victory at which battle halted Germany's progress?

Question Six: The attempt by both sides to outflank the enemy, in September 1914, was known as?

Question Seven: What were the three common methods for digging trenches?

Question Eight: What was placed in front of the trenches in order to improve the defences?

Question Nine: How deep did the trenches eventually become?

Question Ten: What animal were the generals of the First World War often likened to?

HERE ARE THE CORRECT

Q1) Britain, France and Russia

Q2) Germany, Austria-Hungary and the Ottoman Empire

Q3) The Schlieffen Plan

Q4) 70 km

Q5) The Battle of the Marne

Q6) The Race to the Sea

Q7) Entrenching, sapping, and tunnelling

Q8) Barbed wire

Q9) 12 ft

Q10) Donkeys

CHAPTER THREE

Early Attempts at a Truce

A REQUEST FROM THE VATICAN

In the months leading up to Christmas 1914, the war would claim almost one million lives and a war that initially the fighting nations believed would be over in only a few weeks, now appeared to have no end in sight. With the loss of life increasing, early attempts at a truce were made by each side, but to no avail.

A call for peace had also come from the Vatican, with Pope Benedict XV suggesting that there might be a Christmas truce in December. However, an official cease fire had quickly been dismissed.

* * *

Pope Benedict was elected pontiff on the 3rd September, 1914, only a month after the war had begun. As early as the 1st November, 1914, he issued an encyclical, Ad Beatissimi Apostolorum, appealing for peace:

"The combatants are the greatest and wealthiest nations of the earth; what wonder, then, if, well provided with the most awful weapons modern military science has devised, they strive to destroy one another with refinements of horror. There is no limit to the measure of ruin and of slaughter; day by day the earth is drenched with newly-shed blood, and is covered with the bodies of the wounded and of the slain.

The Christmas Truce of 1914

Who would imagine as we see them thus filled with hatred of one another, that they are all of one common stock, all of the same nature, all members of the same human society?"

In early December, 1914, after the horrors of the First Battle of Ypres had taken place, the pope then called for a truce at Christmas, pleading that the nations "cease the clang of arms while Christendom celebrates the Feast of the World's Redemption". Unfortunately, this plea from Rome was ignored. Instead, the generals of both sides looked to strongly discourage any notion of a cease fire over the Christmas period.

CRACKDOWN BY THE GENERALS

The British generals had long been wary of the possibility of fraternising occurring between the enemy soldiers, due to the very nature of trench warfare and the fact that the opposing troops were in such close proximity for long periods of time. On the 5th December 1914, as Christmas was approaching, General Sir Horace Smith-Dorrien sent out a stark warning to the senior officers in the British army:

"It is during this period that the greatest danger to the morale of troops exists. Experience of this and of every other war proves undoubtedly that troops in trenches in close proximity to the enemy slide very easily, if permitted to do so, into a "live and let live" theory of life... officers and men sink into a military lethargy from which it is difficult to arouse them when the moment for great sacrifices again arises... the attitude of our troops can be readily understood and to a certain extent commands sympathy... such an attitude is however most dangerous for it discourages initiative in commanders and destroys the offensive spirit in all ranks".

Smith-Dorrien then went one further by instructing the Divisional Commanders to impress on the subordinate commanders, "the absolute necessity of encouraging offensive spirit... friendly intercourse with the enemy, unofficial armistices, however tempting and amusing they may be, are absolutely prohibited".

Nonetheless, unofficial truces in certain places along the Western Front were attempted. Letters by some soldiers, sent home to loved ones, were later reported in local newspapers throughout Britain, and they told the story of these unofficial truces.

For example, on the 20th December 1914, there was a report of Germans taking in British wounded from no man's land. There were also reports of contact between certain British and German troops lasting all morning, however, equally there were reports of British soldiers getting killed by rifle fire, while assisting the wounded.

From reports that appeared later in the German newspapers, it appears that on the 23rd December 1914 both the Germans and the British had already been heard singing hymns in the trenches, while many German reinforcements coming to the frontline brought little Christmas trees with them, which they placed on top of the parapets of the trenches. There may even have been some local truces on the 23rd December, but these were few and far between.

Did you know?

Despite his tough stance against any type of fraternisation with the enemy, General Smith-Dorrien was actually quite fair to the ordinary soldier, creating many popular reforms during his career.

He was able to speak to troops with ease and was admired by regimental officers.

TRUCES THROUGH THE AGES

Although by far the most well known unofficial war-time truce, the Christmas Truce of 1914 was by no means a one-off. Other informal truces and small armistices have taken place through the ages, when the opposing troops were in close proximity for prolonged periods of time.

Below are some other lesser-known war time truces that took place prior to the Christmas Truce of 1914:

The Peninsular War (1808-1814)

The Peninsular War, which actually formed part of the Napoleonic Wars, was a military conflict between France and the allied powers of Spain, Portugal and Great Britain. Originally, Spain was allied to France, and had allowed Napoleon to send his army through Spain to invade Portugal. However, once his troops were in place in Spain, Napoleon usurped the Spanish king and put his brother, Joseph, on the throne.

* * *

David James Ault

During the war in Portugal, the French and British lines were so close at times that they were forced to get water at the same river, which separated them. Due to this, both sets of soldiers came to an understanding, where they would not fire on one another when fetching water. This then led to incidences of the enemy exchanging gifts and even playing cards around campfires.

The British commander, the Duke of Wellington, was apparently well aware that these activities were taking place between the British and French troops and was quite outraged. He attempted to put a halt to any such type of fraternising, by making it punishable by death for any soldier to have any contact of this sort with the enemy.

* * *

The Christmas Truce of 1914

The Crimean War (1853–1856)

The Crimean War was a war fought by Russia against France, Britain and the Ottoman Empire, between October 1853 and February 1856. The conflict began over the rights of the Christian minorities in the Holy Lands, where the French promoted the rights of Catholics, while Russia promoted those of the Orthodox Christians. However, the main reason for the war, which Russia eventually lost, was the simple fact that Britain and France did not want to see Russia seize new territory at the expense of a declining Ottoman Empire.

A first hand account of the Crimean War, which was published in the New York Times, in April 1883, tells of fraternising between Russian and French soldiers, in the valley of Tchernaya, which had become a sort of neutral ground between the armies.

"Communications were soon established between them by signals at the advanced posts. A French sentry would tie his pocket-handkerchief on his bayonet, and a Russian sentry would leave a bottle of vodka, or brandy, at the end of his beat. In the evening a comrade not on guard would go to the spot, and, taking the bottle, would put a couple of loaves of white bread in its place".

This system of white flags gradually developed into a long practice of short armistices under flags of truce.

The Second Boer War (1899-1902)

The Christmas Truce of 1914 was not even the first time that a football match was played between enemy soldiers. That particular honour goes to a game reportedly played between the British and the Boers, during the Second Boer War.

Sunday truces were already common place during the war, because the Boers abstained from fighting due to religious reasons. Furthermore, a truce also took place on Christmas Day and Boxing Day in 1899, at Mafeking.

TEST YOUR KNOWLEDGE IN THE

What have you learnt about the Early Attempts at a Truce?

(N.B. The answers are shown on the following page)

Question One: Which pope called for a Christmas Truce in December 1914?

Question Two: What encyclical did the pope issue?

Question Three: The horrors of which battle led to the pope's call for a truce?

Question Four: Which British General sent out a stark

warning against fraternisation?

Question Five: What did many of the German reinforcements bring to the frontline with them in December 1914?

Question Six: The Peninsular War was fought between France and which three allied powers?

Question Seven: Who made it punishable by death for a British soldier to fraternise with the French?

Question Eight: In the Crimean War, the French and Russians worked out a system of flags for their short armistices. What colour were they?

Question Nine: In what war was the first football match played between enemy soldiers?

Question Ten: On what day of the week did the Boers abstain from fighting?

HERE ARE THE CORRECT

Q1) Pope Benedict XV

Q2) Ad Beatissimi Apostolorum

Q3) First Battle of Ypres

Q4) General Sir Horace Smith-Dorrien

Q5) Little Christmas trees

Q6) Spain, Portugal and the United Kingdom

Q7) The Duke of Wellington

Q8) White

Q9) The Second Boer War

Q10) Sunday

CHAPTER FOUR

The Christmas Truce of 1914

CHRISTMAS EVE

In the lead up to Christmas, a high volume of mail and gifts were sent to the troops at the front from Great Britain and Germany. King George V sent out a Christmas card to every British soldier, sailor and nurse, while Kaiser Wilhelm II sent little Christmas Trees to the German soldiers to put up in their trenches.

King George V's only daughter, Princess Mary, was very active during the war and helped set up a number of projects to give comfort to British servicemen and assistance to their families. One of Princess Mary's projects was the Christmas Gift Fund, through which £100,000 worth of gifts were sent out to the British soldiers and sailors fighting in the war.

These cards, gifts and Christmas trees, as well as the letters and photos from loved ones, were sent in the hope that the soldiers would feel the spirit of Christmas, however small. The weather would also play its part in achieving that goal, when on Christmas Eve a hard frost helped to make the conditions in the trenches a little more bearable.

Despite all the gifts and letters that were sent out and the fact that Christmas Eve had arrived, it first appeared that the war was to continue as normal. Indeed, back in England, a German aeroplane dropped a bomb on Dover, which just so happened to be the first ever air raid in British history. It is believed that the actual target had been Dover Castle, which was being used as a military base at the time, but the bomb landed in a garden near Taswell Street, in Dover, blowing a gardener out of a tree and leaving a 10 ft-wide crater.

Back on the Western Front, there was sniper fire and deaths on both sides in the morning, but then during the early evening, the first signs of a seasonal goodwill appear when the British soldiers look out over no man's land, only to see Christmas trees with candles lighting up the parapets on the German trenches. This incredible sight is accompanied with the singing of carols and hymns by the Germans, which the British reciprocate in turn.

The first attempts at communication between the enemy also begin along the front, starting with Christmas messages being shouted out by both sides. This is followed by more practical communications concerning local cease fires taking place, in order to collect bodies from no man's land and to bury the dead. However, despite this, in some places along the front, sniper fire continues regardless.

Did you know?

Princess Mary's gift boxes included boiled sweets, chocolate, cigarettes and even a pencil made from a .303 shell casing, along with a printed note that read:

"With best wishes for a victorious New Year from the Princess Mary and friends at home."

CHRISTMAS DAY

The seasonal goodwill experienced along the Western Front on Christmas Eve, continued through the night into Christmas Day, where soldiers on both sides began to shout out to the enemy that they wanted to meet up in no man's land and wish each other a Merry Christmas.

It must have been incredibly nerve racking for the first brave souls to venture out over the top, from the relative safety of the trenches, but gradually more and more soldiers joined in this extraordinary event, in numerous places all along the front, and made the journey to meet up with the enemy.

First-hand reports from the soldiers, on both sides, who took part in the Christmas Truce of 1914, tell of the surreal experience of meeting and shaking hands with the very people they had been trying to kill only a few days before.

Although the unofficial truce did not take place everywhere, it is believed that more than half of the British forces took part in one way or another, with soldiers exchanging news and stories with their fellow man, some even swapping addresses. Presents and small gifts were also exchanged, with cigarettes, cigars, alcohol and food all changing hands, as well as souvenirs and keepsakes, such as buttons and hats.

Letters from the British soldiers that took part, some of which would eventually be printed in local newspapers up and down the country, are a wonderful insight into the events that took place during the truce. Letters such as the one written by Rifleman C.H. Brazier, which was published in the Hertfordshire Mercury, on the 9th January 1915:

"On Christmas Eve the Germans entrenched opposite us began calling out to us 'Cigarettes', 'Pudding', 'A Happy Christmas' and 'English – means good', so two of our fellows climbed over the parapet of the trench and went towards the German trenches. Half-way they were met by four Germans, who said they would not shoot on Christmas Day if we did not. They gave our fellows cigars and a bottle of wine and were given a cake and cigarettes. When they came back I went out with some more of our fellows and we were met by about 30 Germans, who seemed to be very nice fellows. I got one of them to write his name and address on a postcard as a souvenir. All through the night we sang carols to them and they sang to us and one played 'God Save the King' on a mouth organ."

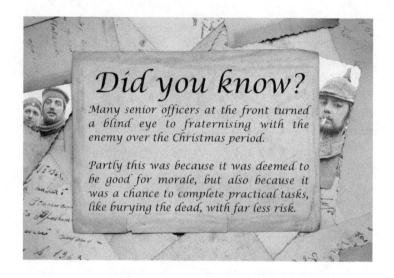

BOXING DAY TO THE NEW YEAR

There were also reports from professional writers who experienced the Christmas Truce first hand, such as Captain Bruce Bairnsfather, the prominent British humorist and cartoonist, who wrote:

"I wouldn't have missed that unique and weird Christmas Day for anything. ... I spotted a German officer, some sort of lieutenant I should think, and being a bit of a collector, I intimated to him that I had taken a fancy to some of his buttons. ... I brought out my wire clippers and, with a few deft snips, removed a couple of his buttons and put them in my pocket. I then gave him two of mine in exchange. ... The last I saw was one of my machine gunners, who was a bit of an amateur hairdresser in civil life, cutting the unnaturally long hair of a docile Boche, who was patiently kneeling on the ground whilst the automatic clippers crept up the back of his neck."

In some areas along the Western Front, the Christmas spirit continued into Boxing Day, but for the majority of troops there was certainly a feeling of an inevitable return to arms, which was summed up perfectly in a letter from Private C Rands - B Company, 2nd Northamptonshire Regiment, which was published on the 2nd January 1915, in the Croydon Advertiser and East Surrey Reporter:

"If you were all out here you would never think we were at war, but still it won't be like this for long, only over the holidays... The war is jolly fine if it's like this all the time, but I expect by the time you get this we shall be shooting at them again for all we are worth".

Meanwhile, although the senior officers at the front had taken rather a pragmatic view towards the truce, news of the fraternisation with the enemy had got back to HQ, who were determined to put an end to such behaviour. Certainly, incidences of open fraternisation soon disappeared all along the front, but nonetheless a relaxed atmosphere remained for several days afterwards, with little or no firing from either side.

* * *

The Christmas Truce of 1914

In some places along the Western Front there was even a truce of some sort on New Year's Eve. Songs were sung and salvos were fired into the air at midnight, but fraternising did not take place to the same extent as during the Christmas Truce.

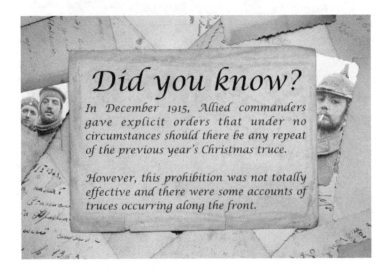

Did you know?

In December 1915, Allied commanders gave explicit orders that under no circumstances should there be any repeat of the previous year's Christmas truce.

However, this prohibition was not totally effective and there were some accounts of truces occurring along the front.

TEST YOUR KNOWLEDGE IN THE

What have you learnt about the Christmas Truce of 1914?

(N.B. The answers are shown on the following page)

Question One: What did King George V send out to every British soldier, sailor and nurse?

Question Two: What did Kaiser Wilhelm send to the German soldiers?

Question Three: What did Princess Mary's gift boxes contain?

Question Four: What type of weather on Christmas Eve

helped make conditions in the trenches a little more bearable?

Question Five: What was the target of the first ever air raid on British soil?

Question Six: What did the Germans put up on the parapets of their trenches?

Question Seven: What types of small gifts did the British and Germans exchange?

Question Eight: What types of souvenirs did the British and Germans exchange?

Question Nine: What are a wonderful insight into the events that took place during the truce?

Question Ten: What was the name of the prominent British humorist and cartoonist, who took part in the Christmas Truce?

HERE ARE THE CORRECT

Q1) A Christmas card

Q2) Little Christmas trees

Q3) Chocolate and cigarettes

Q4) A hard frost

Q5) Dover Castle

Q6) Christmas trees with candles

Q7) Cigarettes, cigars, alcohol and food

Q8) Buttons and hats

Q9) Letters from the soldiers that took part

Q10) Captain Bruce Bairnsfather

CHAPTER FIVE

The Football Match

THE FOOTBALL BATTALION

Towards the end of the 19th Century, there was a lot of debate in Great Britain, as to whether football should become a professional sport or remain an amateur game. Players in Scotland and Northern England could not afford to miss work to play football and so pushed for a professional sport, while the mainly middle-class players of the Southern England teams preferred the Corinthian values of an amateur game.

Those clubs pushing for football to become a professional sport got their wish, with the Football Association finally legalising professionalism in 1885. Then just three years later, in 1888, the Football League was established and with it the popularity of the game began to grow considerably.

When war broke out, in August 1914, professional footballers were often unable to "answer the call" and join up to fight, unless they had permission from the owners of their particular club, as they were not allowed to simply break their contracts. Even so, many amateur players did volunteer to fight for their country right at the start of the war, and some professionals were allowed to join them too.

Among the early volunteers were the entire Heart of Midlothian team, who helped form a volunteer battalion, which eventually became the 16th Royal Scots. Then on the 12th December 1914, the 17th Service Battalion of the Middlesex Regiment was formed, and by March 1915, a total of 122 professional footballers had signed up, which led it to be commonly known as the Football Battalion. Among these early recruits, were the entire Clapton Orient team (later to be known as Leyton Orient).

* * *

Despite these cases of early volunteers, the majority of professional footballers remained with their clubs in the 1914/1915 season, where they were first considered to be a welcome distraction from the war. However, football did begin to play its part in the war effort when, during the early games in that season, the matches were used to try and shame the fans into signing up to fight in the war.

This recruitment drive was actually achieved by printing photos of the crowds at football matches, showing men in civilian clothes next to soldiers in their uniforms. These early "propaganda posters" had headlines cajoling the men, asking if they were not ashamed to be standing dressed in civilian clothes next to a brave man dressed in khaki.

Did you know?

A total of sixteen players from Heart of Midlothian Football Club enlisted in the new volunteer battalion, joining together on the 25th November 1914, to fight for their country.

Unfortunately, seven first team players never returned.

BRAVE FOOTBALLERS REMEMBERED

Although there was an initial push by the clubs for professional football to continue, in order to keep the public's spirits up, opinion soon turned against the professional footballers, as reports of casualties started coming in from the front. Sir Arthur Conan Doyle appealed for footballers to volunteer for service, saying "If a footballer has strength of limb, let them serve and march in the field of battle".

Many people who had lost a loved one to the war were now quite upset to see these fit, able-bodied young men running around a football pitch, instead of fighting for their country against the Germans. It even got to the stage that there were calls for King George V to cease being a patron of The Football Association.

As conscription was not actually introduced in Britain until January 1916, it was still up to the individual footballers as to whether or not they wanted to volunteer to fight in the war. However, when the Football League was disbanded in 1915, more and more footballers began to answer the call. From the 5,000 or so men playing professional football in Great Britain, in 1914, approximately 2,000 joined military service.

Quite a number of the professional footballers fighting in World War I received medals for bravery, including the following players who all received the Victoria Cross: Bernard Vann (Derby County), Donald Simpson Bell

The Christmas Truce of 1914

(Newcastle United) and William Angus (Celtic).

Some professional footballers were recommended for medals of bravery, but never actually received them; perhaps the most famous of these was Walter Tull.

Walter played for Spurs between 1909-11, before joining Northampton Town. When the war broke out, he left "The Cobblers" to enlist in the army, in December of 1914.

Such was Tull's bravery during the war, especially during the Battle of the Somme, that he became the first mixed-race combat officer in the British Army, despite the fact that the 1914 Manual of Military Law explicitly excluded mixed-raced soldiers from command as officers.

Unfortunately, Second Lieutenant Walter Tull was killed in

action on the 25th March 1918, during the Spring Offensive. One of the many brave footballers, who laid down their lives for King and Country during the Great War.

Did you know?

Walter Tull was the second black player to play professionally in Britain and was one of fourteen players with Tottenham Hotspur connections, who died in WWI.

Unfortunately, whilst playing for Spurs, he was often racially abused by the opposition's supporters.

FOOTBALL IN THE CHRISTMAS TRUCE

Although there is no question that there was a Christmas Truce between Great Britain and Germany in 1914, there are many historians who doubt whether an organised football match actually took place between the two sides. The football match has, in many ways, become the symbol of the Christmas Truce of 1914, but did it really take place?

The easy answer to that question is that it is quite hard to say one way or another. The historical evidence consists mainly of letters from British and German soldiers at the time, as well as accounts from veteran soldiers many years later. However, this 'evidence' is mainly made up by second hand accounts of soldiers writing about a football match that they had heard was going to take place or had taken place, rather than first hand accounts of soldiers who either played or watched an actual game. Then there are also the first hand accounts, which have later proven to be fake.

Whether there was an actual organised game in no-man's land between the British and Germans is still open to debate and it is quite hard to prove one way or the other. However, there is no doubt that football had become the people's game by that time and so the likelihood of impromptu kick-abouts between British and German soldiers along the Western Front is very high.

* * *

The question that should be asked is, why is it that a football match has emerged as the overriding symbol of the Christmas Truce, rather than the Christmas carol or even the Christmas tree? After all, they would appear to be far more deserving examples of a symbol for the Christmas Truce of 1914, albeit a little less romantic.

Perhaps the answer to this question is quite a simple one. One hundred years on from the Christmas Truce, football is still very much the people's game and is something that today's generation can easily relate to. So does it really matter if it is possible to prove that an organised football match took place or not during the truce? Surely, it is more important that the young generation of today understands the spirit of the truce, and thus if a football match helps to achieve that goal, then that can only be a good thing.

TEST YOUR KNOWLEDGE IN THE

What have you learnt about the Football Match?

(N.B. The answers are shown on the following page)

Question One: Players in which parts of the country pushed for football to become a professional sport?

Question Two: In what year did the Football Association finally legalise professionalism in football?

Question Three: In what year was the Football League established?

Question Four: Whose permission did the professional footballers need if they wanted to "answer the call" and join up to fight in the war?

Question Five: What did the 17th Service Battalion of the Middlesex Regiment become known as?

Question Six: When was conscription introduced in Britain?

Question Seven: Approximately how many professional footballers joined the military service?

Question Eight: What did Walter Tull become the first ever in the British army?

Question Nine: On what date was Walter Tull killed in action during the Spring Offensive?

Question Ten: What was Walter Tull's rank when he died?

HERE ARE THE CORRECT

Q1) Scotland and Northern England

Q2) 1885

Q3) 1888

Q4) Their football club's owners

Q5) The Football Battalion

Q6) January 1916

Q7) 2,000

Q8) The first mixed-race combat officer

Q9) 25th March 1918

Q10) Second Lieutenant

CHAPTER SIX

Centenary of the Truce

THE LEGACY OF THE TRUCE

History is a wonderful thing in that it not only gives us a chance to learn from our mistakes in the past, but also to champion those occasions when the human race does something to be truly proud of. At the time, Sir Arthur Conan Doyle referred to the Christmas Truce as "one human episode amid all the atrocities, which have stained the memory of the war". He was right.

It is clear from the news articles and letters from the front at the time, just what an impact the Christmas Truce had on the human psyche. The soldiers who took part in the truce were themselves amazed that they were suddenly exchanging gifts and pleasantries with the same men they had been shooting at just the day before. It must have been a surreal experience to say the least.

However, the Christmas Truce was not actually reported in the newspapers to begin with, as there was an unofficial press embargo that held back on reporting the news. Eventually, the embargo was broken by the New York Times on the 31st December, and following this the British papers also started to print stories of the truce, including numerous first-hand accounts from soldiers at the front.

Meanwhile, in Germany there was far less coverage in the papers, with many articles strongly criticising those that took part. In France, there was no coverage at all to begin with, due to the stricter censorship of the press. When a report did finally come out, it was in the form of a government notice, warning that fraternising with the enemy constituted treason.

Perhaps this negative cloud that initially covered the truce was the reason that it was hardly mentioned much at all in the years following the war. Indeed, it was not until the 1960's that references to the Christmas Truce first began appearing in the media; in the song, "Snoopy's Christmas", and a scene in the musical film, "Oh! What a Lovely War".

However, it was not until the eighties and nineties that the Christmas Truce really gained public attention, in songs such as Paul McCartney's "Pipes of Peace", The Farm's "All Together Now" and the wonderful "Christmas in the Trenches", by John McCutcheon.

* * *

Did you know?

One of the earliest references to the Christmas Truce in the media was in 1933, where it was shown in a negative light.

In a play written by the Nazi writer, Heinz Steguweit, a German soldier is shot dead by the enemy, whilst decorating a Christmas tree between the trenches.

EVENTS TO MARK THE CENTENARY

By the turn of the century, more and more references to the Christmas Truce were now appearing in the media, in the lead up to the Centenary of the First World War.

In 2005, the film "Joyeux Noël" actually depicted a fictionalised account of the truce, through the eyes of French, Scottish and German soldiers. Then, on the 11th November 2008, a Christmas Truce memorial was unveiled in the small village of Frelinghien, situated on the Franco-Belgian frontier.

British and German descendants of Great War veterans, in period uniforms, shake hands at the unveiling of a memorial to the truce on

The Christmas Truce of 1914

*11 November 2008 in Frelinghien, France (*Used under Creative Commons 2.0 *by Alan Cleaver).*

Also on the 11th November 2008, The Royal Welch Fusiliers played a football match with the German Battalion 371 at the spot where their regimental ancestors had came out from their trenches, on Christmas Day 1914, to play a game of football. The Germans won the match 2–1.

Then, in 2014, there were a series of events throughout the United Kingdom to mark the Centenary of the Christmas Truce and also to commemorate World War 1. These events began as early as May 2014, when a Football Remembers education pack, arranged and supported by the Premier League, The Football Association, the Football League and the British Council, was sent out to more than 30,000 schools across the country.

Included as part of this project was a UK-wide competition to design a Football Remembers memorial to the World War One Christmas Truce. The competition was won by a ten-year-old schoolboy, called Spencer Turner, and the memorial was unveiled in December 2014, at the National Memorial Arboretum in Staffordshire, by Prince William, Duke of Cambridge, and the England football manager, Roy Hodgson.

Another event organised under the umbrella of Football Remembers, was a game played between British and German forces at Aldershot Town's football stadium, on the 17th

December 2014. Aldershot is known as the "Home of the British Army", and so was considered to be a very suitable venue for the match to take place. The British soldiers ended up winning the game 1-0.

UEFA also commemorated the special part that football may have played in the truce with a memorial service in Belgium, where a sculpture was unveiled by UEFA President, Michel Platini. A video was also created by UEFA to remember the Christmas Truce, featuring footballers from Great Britain, France and Germany.

Such was the media coverage of the truce in 2014, and in particular the football match, that the supermarket giant, Sainsbury's, also shot a high quality short film based on the truce for their Christmas advert that year. The 3 minute 40 second advert was made in partnership with The Royal British Legion and was inspired by the events that took place during the Christmas Truce of 1914.

Although the cinematography of the advert, which centred around a moment of friendship and a bar of chocolate between a British and German soldier, was quite outstanding, Sainsbury's immediately came under fire, being accused of exploiting the Christmas Truce and disrespecting the memory of those soldiers who lay down their lives during World War One.

Despite the complaints that flooded in following Sainsbury's

The Christmas Truce of 1914

depiction of the truce, there is no doubt that it played its part, along with UEFA and the Football Remembers project, in educating an entire nation about a wonderful event that took place a century before. A single human episode amid all the atrocities that this generation shall always remember.

TEST YOUR KNOWLEDGE IN THE

What have you learnt about the Centenary of the Truce?

(N.B. The answers are shown on the following page)

Question One: Who described the Christmas Truce as "one human episode amid all the atrocities, which have stained the memory of the war"?

Question Two: Which newspaper broke the unofficial press embargo on the Christmas Truce?

Question Three: In which country did the papers not cover the truce?

Question Four: In 2005, which film was based on a

fictionalised account of the truce, through the eyes of French, Scottish and German soldiers?

Question Five: On the 11th November 2008, a Christmas Truce memorial was unveiled in which small village on the Franco-Belgian border?

Question Six: What was the score between the Royal Welch Fusiliers and the German Battalion 371?

Question Seven: How many schools in the UK received the Football Remembers education pack?

Question Eight: The video created by UEFA to remember the Christmas Truce, featured footballers from which countries?

Question Nine: What is the town of Aldershot known as?

Question Ten: What supermarket chain courted controversy with their advert about the Christmas Truce?

HERE ARE THE CORRECT

Q1) Sir Arthur Conan Doyle

Q2) The New York Times

Q3) France

Q4) Joyeux Noël

Q5) Frelinghien

Q6) The Germans won 2-1

Q7) 30,000

Q8) Great Britain, France and Germany

Q9) The Home of the British Army

Q10) Sainsbury's

CHAPTER SEVEN

And finally...

If you have enjoyed reading

**The Real Story of the 1914
Christmas Truce**

then please take the time to leave a

REVIEW

It really would mean a lot to me

Thank you